D1373382

GETTING THE JOB
YOU NEED

GETTING A JOB IN
SANITATION

SUSAN MEYER

ROSEN
PUBLISHING®

NEW YORK

Published in 2014 by The Rosen Publishing Group, Inc.
29 East 21st Street, New York, NY 10010

First Edition

Library of Congress Cataloging-in-Publication Data

Meyer, Susan, 1986-.
Getting a job in sanitation/by Susan Meyer.—1st ed.—New York : Rosen, c2014
    p. cm.—(Job basics: getting the job you need)
Includes bibliographical references and index.
ISBN 978-1-4488-9607-3
1. Sanitary engineering—Vocational guidance—Juvenile literature. 2. Refuse and refuse disposal—Vocational guidance—Juvenile literature. 3. Environmental engineering—Vocational guidance—Juvenile literature. 4. Vocational guidance—Juvenile literature. I. Title.
TD156.M49 2014
628.4'023—M5751

Manufactured in the United States of America

CPSIA Compliance Information: Batch #S13YA: For further information, contact Rosen Publishing, New York, New York, at 1-800-237-9932.

CONTENTS

INTRODUCTION

When you think about people who work in the community to keep it running smoothly, you might first think of police officers and firefighters who keep people safe. Or you might think of postal workers and crossing guards who provide important services to the community and its citizens. However, one job you might overlook that is essential to your community's smooth running and well-being—whether you live in a huge city, a suburban neighborhood, or a small town— is that of the sanitation worker.

You've likely noticed garbage trucks rumbling around your neighborhood a couple of times a week, but if they do their job correctly, you might not give them another thought. However, if they stop doing their job, you notice very quickly. Americans fill sixty-three thousand garbage trucks full of trash each year. That's enough trucks to stretch from Earth halfway to the moon! Someone has to fill these trucks and drive them away to dispose of trash safely in landfills.

Without modern sanitation, life as we know it would be very different. Garbage and scraps would sit on the streets creating foul odors. Worse still, this accumulating waste would spread diseases. It would be particularly bad in large cities. In the 1800s, before an official program of sanitation and street cleaning was put into effect, New York was one of the dirtiest cities in the world. By 1832, there were reports that New

Sanitation workers perform an incredibly important function for people around the country. They remove an average of 250 million tons of solid waste each year, keeping our cities and towns clean and safe to live in.

York smelled so bad that travelers 6 miles (9.7 km) away could rely on their noses to tell them when they were approaching the city. Diseases that today are nearly unheard of in the United States—like cholera and dysentery—were frequent visitors to the Big Apple. The average lifespan for people in the city at that time was only forty years—comparable to that of medieval, plague-ravaged London. It wasn't until 1903, when the city adopted a system of sanitation and trash collection, that people's health and well-being began to improve.

Organized sanitation and trash collecting isn't just important in cities. Today, sanitation workers collect trash in cities, towns, and suburbs all across the country. Sanitation workers aren't just the men and women you see driving or loading the trucks. Some sanitation workers are in charge of operations in landfills, while others organize the movement of trucks from offices.

All of these men and women have a tough job. The average day for sanitation workers usually begins long before the sun is up and continues until their route is complete and all the trash in their assigned area is collected. It can be a dangerous and smelly job, but it is also incredibly important. Because of the vital role they play in the community, sanitation workers receive good benefits and salary. The job is difficult and is certainly not for everyone, but it can be a great way to make a good living.

The Trash Trade

Trash. Garbage. Refuse. Waste. Regardless of what it is called, we produce a lot of it. In fact, the average American produces 29 pounds (13 kg) of trash every single week! Someone has to remove this waste from people's homes to where it can be disposed of safely. "Sanitation worker" is the official name for the person who performs this important task.

Sanitation workers maintain and operate various types of equipment involved in street cleaning, waste collection, recycling collection, waste disposal, and, sometimes, snow removal. These workers follow an assigned route that tells them exactly where their work area is. They follow this route and load and unload waste materials. Sometimes they will manually empty trashcans. Other times they will operate the machinery that allows the truck itself to lift and empty residential garbage cans and large dumpsters. Sanitation workers also monitor the collected waste for hazardous or toxic materials. They sweep and clean city streets, usually with specially designed vehicles.

In many places, sanitation workers may also be in charge of a citywide recycling program and assist in removing millions of pounds of materials to be brought to recycling plants. During winter months in northern climates, they attach and operate snowplows, remove snow and ice from city streets and important roadways, and spread salt and sand to make

In many places, sanitation workers don't just remove trash. They also transport approved recyclable materials. These materials are taken to a recycling plant where they can be melted down and reused.

driving safer for everyone. In some cities and towns, sanitation workers also perform tasks like removing debris from vacant lots and collecting abandoned cars, other vehicles, and furniture. Not only do they perform these highly visible everyday tasks, but, behind the scenes, some sanitation workers are also in charge of preparing reports, entering data, and maintaining records. As you can see, there's a lot more to being a sanitation worker than you might think.

There are many different jobs available within and throughout the sanitation industry. Some of these involve working for the state or local government. These public workers do everything from driving trucks and loading garbage into them to monitoring vehicle routes, running city or state landfills, and handling overall logistics to help collect the community's trash.

Not all sanitation workers work for governments and municipalities, however. Some are employed by private waste collection facilities.

Landfills are not only places to dump trash far away from people. Some landfills, such as this one in New Jersey, are equipped to gather the methane gas produced by garbage and turn it into a source of energy.

Some of these private companies operate in towns where there is no public waste collection. This means that customers pay these companies on a weekly, monthly, or annual basis to keep their trash from piling up. Hiring someone to do it means that they don't have to make the trip to a dump or landfill themselves. Other private companies are paid to remove the trash from commercial businesses. Sometimes these businesses produce specialized or hazardous waste that requires extra care when removing it and hauling it away.

ON STRIKE!

In major cities, where many people live close together, sanitation strikes can quickly turn into dire situations. In 1911, sanitation workers in New York City went on strike for several weeks. A *New York Times* article described the city just four days after the strike began: "[B]ig piles of garbage, mostly of rotting perishables, were surrounded by playing children and scavenging cats and dogs." Not a pretty picture.

Perhaps the most famous sanitation strike is one that occurred in the city of Memphis, Tennessee, in 1968. At that time, one thousand mostly African American sanitation workers went on strike to demand higher wages and safer working conditions from Memphis city officials. What followed was a series of sit-ins and nonviolent protests led by civil rights activist Martin Luther King Jr. Tragically, King was assassinated while in Memphis. In the aftermath of the assassination, the sanitation workers were successful in getting the city to recognize their union and give in to some of their demands.

Pros and Cons of the Job

Working in sanitation, though very rewarding in many respects, is not without its drawbacks. It is important to understand both the benefits and the drawbacks before pursuing any career choice. First of all, there is the obvious: trash collection is a smelly job. The work can also be very physically demanding. It can involve both heavy lifting and being on your feet most of the day. It is a year-round job that must be done in all weather, even if it's snowing or raining. If you've ever been woken up by the rumbling of a garbage truck before dawn, you also know that the work begins very early in the

After Hurricane Sandy devastated the East Coast, sanitation workers put in many overtime hours to help with the massive cleanup. These workers are removing debris from the boardwalk in Ocean City, Maryland.

day. Sanitation work is not for people who don't like to get up early. The work day can start as early as four in the morning.

Additionally, the job can be very dangerous. *Business Insider* lists sanitation work as number seven on a list of the fifteen most dangerous jobs in America. The number one cause of death on the job for sanitation workers is due to truck-related accidents. However, there are a number of other on-the-job hazards that can affect workers. First of all, people sometimes throw out things that are dangerous. These include substances that can cause chemical burns, disposable needles, and broken glass. Sanitation workers also have to be on the lookout for falling objects from overloaded containers, diseases that may accompany solid waste, materials and debris containing asbestos, dogs that may attack, and pests (ants, flies, cockroaches, and rodents) that root around in garbage.

Despite these drawbacks, there are also some great advantages to this line of work. For starters, many sanitation workers are employed by the government, whether it is the government of a big city or county or a small town. There are many benefits of working for the government. It often means, in addition to paid vacation, that you will also get government holidays off. Trash collection is also a career with a fair amount of job stability. While the government may cut funding to some programs, as long as people keep producing garbage (and Americans continuing to produce garbage in great quantities is a pretty safe bet), it will have to pay someone to collect it. There are usually opportunities for sanitation workers to put in overtime hours and make extra money. This is especially true after big storms or during winter months when they might be called in to clear storm debris, fallen trees, snow, and ice from roads.

Another advantage of working for the government is a reliable series of raises based on experience. The longer you work as a sanitation worker, the higher your salary will be. Sanitation workers might also be given a retirement plan called a pension. This means that you will save part of your income in a retirement account and the government will match some of those funds. At the end of your career, when you retire, you can live off of that money. Those sanitation workers who are employed by private carting companies may not have the same benefits as those offered in government positions.

Actual salaries for sanitation workers will vary widely by location. They will also depend on whom you work for. However, looking at the average salaries for the middle 50 percent of sanitation workers will give you some idea of the expected compensation. Visit the Web site of the Bureau of Labor Statistics (www.bls.gov) to find the most recent salary information for positions in the sanitation industry.

Ultimately, sanitation work is a tough job, but it can be very rewarding. You get to be part of a team. Also, you are doing a job that provides a real service to people every day. You can go to work knowing that you are making a real difference in the lives of individuals and their communities.

Sanitation Workers United

Depending on the sanitation department or company where you work, you might be required to join a union. A union is an organization of workers who join together to achieve common goals. These goals might include achieving higher pay, increasing the number of workers hired, or improving working conditions. Labor unions have been around in the United States since the early nineteenth century. There was an increase in unions in the 1950s and '60s, especially in public-sector jobs such as sanitation. This was partially because the U.S. government was enjoying the benefits of a strong economy and it could afford to give into union salary demands.

Unions usually select leaders who can represent their members. These leaders bring union demands to the people in management or ownership who are in a position to either grant the requests or negotiate a compromise agreement. Although they generally use it only as a last resort when negotiations halt, unions can threaten to strike to achieve their demands. When workers are out on strike, it means that they are not doing the work that is essential to a company or government and the larger community.

If everyone who knows how to perform a certain job is united and refusing to work, it can put a lot of pressure on management and ownership to settle the disagreement. If a settlement is slow to be made, a lot of money is lost, the

Unions are a way for sanitation workers to join together to use the strength of their numbers. If they organize, sanitation workers are better able to fight for increased pay and benefits and better working conditions.

community suffers, order begins to break down, and citizens become angry. During a sanitation strike, this chaotic situation becomes a reality. To prevent this from happening, the government of a city or town will often try very hard to negotiate in good faith with public service unions and avoid paralyzing work stoppages.

So what are the pros and cons of joining a union? There are a number of advantages to being a union worker. For one,

union members have the benefit of negotiating with their employer as a unified group. This basic right gives them much more power and leverage than if they were to negotiate individually. It means they usually make more money and have better benefits than nonunion workers. However, as a union member, you will be expected to pay dues. These payments help keep the union operating. They are also funneled into a fund that helps pay workers when they are out on strike and not receiving a regular paycheck. Not all sanitation workers are unionized, but you should make learning about your local sanitation union a part of your job research as you consider this career path.

Education and Testing Requirements

One of the advantages of working in the sanitation industry is that most jobs will not require a college degree. If you are not interested in going to college, but are interested in building a career rather than merely getting a job, the sanitation industry is a sensible path to consider. However, even though you may not be college bound, sanitation work still requires you to have a good education. While it is true that the main focus of sanitation work is to collect and properly dispose of trash and other debris, there are aspects of the job that require basic skills in reading, writing, and mathematics.

Workers must be able to carefully read and understand detailed instructions for how complicated machines work. Jobs in the sanitation industry can be very dangerous. Many of the on-the-job injuries are related to machinery and truck accidents. For this reason, excellent reading skills, listening skills, and attention to detail are extremely important. You will also need good writing skills because sometimes sanitation workers are asked to keep notes or logs of their routes. These written records will need to be clear and well maintained because they will usually be shared with your boss. Math skills will also come into play in these records. Sanitation workers might be asked to make calculations based on their work in the field. You will also be expected to read and

Sanitation workers need to have a high school education because reading instructions and maps and maintaining and notating written schedules and records are important parts of their job.

interpret maps in order to learn and follow your assigned route and be able to deviate from it when asked to in special circumstances.

Minimum Requirements

Because the safe and smooth performance of sanitation-related jobs is so important, most cities and towns have a minimum education requirement to ensure that all candidates possess the necessary skills and knowledge to perform the essential tasks. This requirement is usually a high school diploma, a certificate of completion, or a general equivalency diploma (or GED). Some cities and towns also require that sanitation workers fluently speak and understand English. They may have workers who were not born in the United States or in a country where English is the primary language take a test in order to prove their fluency.

Many cities, towns, and municipalities also have a minimum age requirement that must be met in order to apply for any sanitation jobs. While the age varies slightly, most locations set the minimum age at somewhere between eighteen and twenty-one. Visit the sanitation department Web site of the town or city you hope to work for to find out what its minimum age requirement is.

Driver's Licenses and Testing

In addition to the standard education requirements, sanitation workers are also usually required to have a valid driver's license. Workers must be able to learn how to properly and safely operate the machines and trucks associated with the job. This often requires a special driver's license called a commercial driver's license, or CDL.

Driving a garbage truck is very different from driving a normal passenger vehicle. Aspiring sanitation workers must practice driving the truck and pass a test to get their commercial driver's license.

In order to drive sanitation vehicles, you must qualify for a CDL. However, you can often apply and qualify for this type of license after you have already been hired as a sanitation worker. It depends on who hires you, but often you will receive CDL training on the job.

The driver's test necessary to obtain a CDL will involve a hands-on skills test that requires you to demonstrate that you know how to use an air brake—equipped vehicle such as a garbage truck. It is important that you double-check whether or not you need to obtain a CDL before applying to your locality's sanitation department. You may be allowed to train for the licensing test once you are already employed. If the license can be obtained after being hired, you will need to know how long after your start date you have until you will need to pass the licensing test and receive your commercial driver's license.

The Civil Service Exam

In many cities, sanitation workers are hired from a civil service list. The civil service is composed of all public or government workers. Civil service jobs can include everything from firefighters to police officers to sanitation workers. To get on this list, interested parties must take and pass a civil service exam. In addition to a written exam, they may also be asked to pass a physical test.

You can find out if your city uses the civil service list to hire sanitation workers by visiting the Web site for your local department of sanitation. It should list all of the education and other requirements needed in order for an applicant to be considered for an open job. If your city does draw from a civil service list, this Web site should also provide a link to

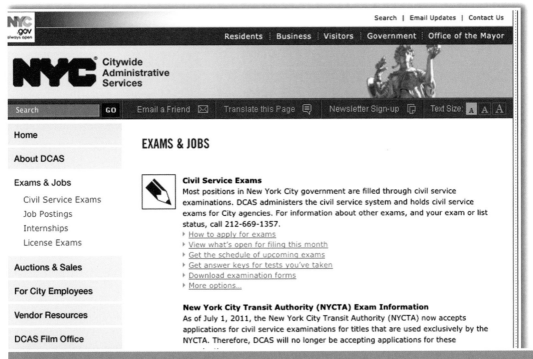

By searching the department of sanitation Web site of your city or town, you may be able to find out not only if the civil service exam is required, but also information on how to sign up for the test and when it is offered. This is New York City's civil service exams and jobs page (www.nyc.gov/html/dcas/html/employment/employ.shtml).

information on how you can apply to take the civil service exam. There are different tests for different jobs. Obviously the test for those interested in becoming a firefighter will be very different from the test to become a sanitation worker.

If the civil service exam is a requirement for sanitation jobs in your area, you might wonder what the best way to prepare for it is. After all, as you've learned in school, the best way to make sure you do well on a test is to be as prepared as possible. The bad news is that the Internet is not the best place to get information on the civil service exam, so you'll need to do some legwork. The reason for this is that most of the government organizations that give these tests don't choose to make study materials or sample questions available online. You may find a study guide for sale online. However, this will likely not be specific to your city or town's test. In rare cases, cities will put some sample test questions online. If you don't have an Internet connection, you can access these resources at your local public library, a community center, the YMCA, or a career or employment assistance center.

While you're at your local library, you can take advantage of some of the other civil service exam materials it may have on hand. While many cities don't put test materials online, many public libraries have recognized the need for their community members to have access to civil service exam study guides. Some have purchased copies of them for their collections. Libraries will often hold these in their reference collection so that they can't be checked out. They do this to ensure that people will be able to use them without competing with others who may already have checked these materials out. Ask a librarian for help in finding guides for the test you are taking, as these can often be tricky to locate through a

The written portion of the civil service exam is just as important as the physical portion of the exam. Read the general instructions and specific questions in your test booklet carefully before offering your answers.

card catalog search. You can also request materials from the organization that is giving the test. It might provide sample questions and test materials, which you can pick up in person or have mailed to you.

There are a number of Web sites online that offer helpful test-taking tips for the civil service exam. However, there are also some general tips you should keep in mind for any important text or exam you may take. Make sure to get a good night's sleep before the day of the exam. Look up the directions to the testing center's location beforehand and figure out how long it will take to get there. Give yourself plenty of time to reach the testing center so that you will not be stressed out when you arrive. Find out what materials you need to bring with you, and don't forget them on the day of the test. Make sure you have plenty of sharpened pencils, just in case one breaks.

The written sanitation workers civil service exam (which varies from municipality to municipality) often covers the following skills, all of which are essential to the work of a sanitation worker: judgment, map reading, math, reading comprehension, spatial relations, and verbal expression. The test is made up of multiple-choice questions. The test is scored on a scale of one to one hundred, and you must score a seventy or above to pass. If you pass the written test, your name is added to an eligibility list for the physical test. In some larger cities, where the pool of applicants is large, not everyone who passes the civil service exam will necessarily be called to take the physical exam. In these cases, a number of people who have passed will be randomly assigned to take the physical exam, and the rest are put on a waiting list.

The physical test consists of a number of trials, each made up of various tasks that are similar to what sanitation workers would really do on the job. These include climbing ladders,

STUDY UP!

Just to get a taste of what the sanitation-related civil service exam might be like, here are a couple of questions modeled after some that appeared in the practical knowledge section of the New York City Sanitation Worker's Exam. Read the questions, write down what you think the answers are on a piece of paper, and then check the bottom to see if you were right:

1) While driving a sweeper, sanitation worker Enrico notices smoke coming out of a window on 1919 Mockingbird Lane. What is the first thing he should do?

A) Stop a person on the street and ask them to call 911.
B) Call in on his radio to tell the dispatcher to call a fire truck.
C) Stop his truck and approach the building to see if anyone is inside and needing help.
D) Drive to the next street to get out of the way because fire trucks will need to move quickly down Mockingbird Lane.

2) Margot is collecting trash in a residential neighborhood, and a bag she is carrying splits open. Four items fall out: a plastic coat hanger, a closed pocket knife, a soldering iron, and a razor blade. Which item is the most dangerous for her to handle?

A) plastic coat hanger   C) soldering iron
B) closed pocket knife   D) razor blade

Answers:
1) B. It will take only seconds to report the fire by radio, and Enrico's actions could save property or even people's lives.
2) D. A razor blade is very sharp and far more likely to cause harm than the other objects.

If you got a question wrong, don't worry about it. By studying test materials and getting a better idea of what the test is asking, you can improve your chances of scoring well.

dragging heavy bins to a garbage truck, emptying bins, and dragging or carrying garbage through an obstacle course.

Assuming you take the written and physical tests and do well on both, what happens next? You will be placed on a list. When the city government needs to hire new sanitation workers, it will draw from this list. The people at the top of the list will be hired first. Once you reach the top of the list, however, you aren't given a job immediately. You still need to pass a medical exam, be able to prove you have a driver's license and possibly a CDL learner's permit, and pass a background check. Sometimes this is all you need to supply before you will be pulled off the waiting list and hired for the next suitable job that becomes available. Other times, depending on the city, town, or municipality in which you are applying, more might be required of you.

Sometimes, in addition to all of this paperwork, testing, licensing, and certification, the person in charge of hiring will need to interview you in person. The interviewer wants to make sure you can do the job, are confident in your abilities and knowledge, and will get along well with the team.

The Job Search

ow that you know a little about what a job in the sanitation industry is like and what skills and education are required of applicants, you might be wondering how to go about finding one of these jobs. Your best friend in this job hunt will be the Internet.

If you don't have home access to a computer or an Internet connection, don't worry. Your local library will likely have computers with Internet access available for public use. You just need to have a valid library card and sign up to use one of the available computers. If there is not a library branch near you, other options for free-to-use computers include YMCAs, community centers, and career assistance centers. In addition to offering Internet access, people working at career assistance centers might also be available to offer you valuable advice during your job search. For example, many of these centers provide résumé review and career counseling. These can come in handy when you reach the application portion of your job search.

Once you're online, it's all about entering the proper search terms into your search engine of choice. A good place to start is your town, city, or county's Web site. You can try searching for its main site and looking for open jobs. You might also try searching your city name followed by "department of sanitation." If your city's department of sanitation has its own Web site or its own page on the main government site, that should come up. Once you're on your city's site, search for "job opportunities" or "job listings." Clicking these buttons should give you access to a list of job openings in your area.

Looking Beyond the Public Sector

Not all sanitation workers are employed by government departments of sanitation. Not everyone who wants to be a sanitation worker for the city is able to because competition for the few available positions can be strong. You can be disqualified from consideration for not doing well on a written exam or for any number of physical or medical reasons. Even if you do meet all the criteria, sometimes there just aren't enough jobs to employ all of the people who would like to work in sanitation.

An alternative is to find employment with a private carting company. These companies collect commercial waste from a city or town's businesses. Anyone in your professional network will

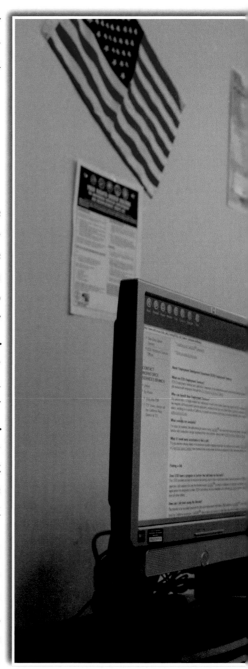

The Internet is an incredibly valuable tool for the modern job search. There are a number of public places where you can access the Internet for free, including schools, libraries, career assistance centers, YMCAs, and community centers.

come in handy here. If anyone you know works for a local business that uses a private waste management company to collect and haul away its garbage, he or she might be able to provide you with the name and contact information for someone at the carting company. If you don't know anyone who has contacts with a private hauling company, you can search for these companies with the help of the Yellow Pages or an Internet search engine. Use search terms like "private carting" or "sanitation services." You should also include your ZIP code (or the ZIP code of the locality where you are seeking employment) to narrow your search to local companies.

Any job listing you find should include a number of helpful details about the job. It should tell you the procedure for applying, as well as the requirements for the position. It may even have a brief description of the job and

This truck is part of Local Rubbish Service, a private sanitation company in Los Angeles, California. While many sanitation jobs are with the government, there are also openings with private companies.

what you will be doing on a daily basis if you are hired. It might give an idea of what the starting salary for the position is. It may include a link to click, taking you to a form you must fill out in order to be considered. Or it might have an e-mail contact for the person to whom you should send your résumé and cover letter. If sanitation workers are required to take the civil service exam in order to be considered, this information will be given in the job listing. It will also detail the steps required to be placed on the civil service list after you have taken the exam. You will usually have to request to

FILLING IT OUT

When you're applying to work for the department of sanitation in the city or town of your choice, you will sometimes be asked to fill out an online application. This application may be for the opportunity to take the civil service exam or it may be to apply directly for a job. Either way, in cases where the application is your only way in, and no résumé or cover letter is required, it is very important to fill out the application very carefully and accurately. If you must apply online and don't have Internet access in your home, try to find a quiet corner of the library or somewhere else free of distractions while you concentrate on completing the application.

You will probably need to gather some materials together before you begin filling out the application. You will need to have your Social Security number. In the case of online applications, it is also a good idea to have your résumé handy. Much of the information you will be required to provide on an online application will be drawn directly from your résumé.

be added to the list and give information like your name and your exam number.

Forming a Network

You may have already noticed that whom you know can be as important as your other qualifications when trying to land a job. In the past, you might have mentioned to your mom that you wanted to make some money, and she helped you out by telling you about a job opening at her friend's grocery store. Or perhaps you mowed the lawn of one of your next-door neighbors, and he recommended your services to another neighbor a few houses down. Having people on your side can be an invaluable tool for getting a job in any industry. It can help you get a foot in the door. Then it's up to you to push that door open, walk in, and take your place within the workplace.

The process of using your personal and professional connections to help you find a job, provide you with information about an industry, or further your career is called networking. You already have a network of people that can help you: your family, teachers, coaches, counselors, neighbors, and community leaders. These people will be happy to offer you advice and leads as you pursue your job search. That's the network you already have, but you can also look for ways to increase your connections.

If you are looking for a job in a specific industry, such as sanitation, the best people to talk to are the ones who work in that industry. If you know people who work in sanitation, they will be a great resource. They can not only tell you about job openings and possibly recommend you to their

Someone who works in the industry can give you valuable information about what a career in sanitation is really like on a day-to-day basis. He or she can also use his or her professional connections to help you find a position.

bosses and supervisors, but they can also provide valuable information about what the job is like on a day-to-day basis.

If you can't immediately think of someone you know who works in the sanitation industry, don't give up hope! You might be connected to someone in the industry without yet realizing it. The best way to uncover connections in your network is to talk to friends, family, and people in your community. Express your interest in working in sanitation and ask them if they know of anyone who can talk to you about it. After talking to your immediate network, try casting your net a little wider. You might want to try talking to people in your community whom you don't know. People at government agencies that specialize in employment can give you valuable advice. You might also contact your local department of sanitation and see if it can offer you any information or allow you to talk to someone to help answer some of your questions.

Looking for work can be a full-time job in itself. Networking, informational interviews, old-fashioned pounding the pavement, and lots and lots of Internet research are required to get that all-important job interview and that dream job.

The one thing you should not do is try to talk to sanitation workers while they are on the job. It might seem like an easy way to make a contact with someone who knows the ins and outs of the job. Remember, however, that when you see sanitation workers driving their trucks on the street, they are at work. They are doing an important and frequently dangerous job. They can't afford to be distracted from the task at hand and may not be too happy to be interrupted. It is much better to go through other avenues to make connections in the industry.

Applying for Jobs

Once you have talked to some people in your network and have decided that you are definitely interested in applying for a job as a sanitation worker, your work is far from over. You will still need to apply all of your research and networking to actually gaining employment. It may be helpful to make a checklist of all the things you will need to do. Staying organized is the best way to make sure no part of your application falls through the cracks. If you know you will have to take a civil service exam as part of your application, write down the test date for both the written and physical exam. If you have a contact person to whom you are sending a résumé, make sure to write down his or her name and contact information.

Many local sanitation departments have an online application that you submit directly via their Web sites. There may be a fee for submitting the application, but usually only in cases where you are applying to take the civil service exam. This fee, usually around $30, can be waived if you are on public assistance. Once your basic application is approved, you will be able to take the civil service exam. Sometimes the online application is for a job itself, not just for the opportunity to take a civil service exam. Smaller cities and private carting companies often ask applicants to send their application materials to a specific contact person. You will have to send this person (via either e-mail or conventional mail) a cover letter and résumé and possibly a completed application form.

Résumés and Cover Letters

Your résumé, sometimes called a curriculum vitae, or CV, is a summary of all of your professional accomplishments. It should list what jobs you have had and what skills you developed and what duties you performed in those positions. The résumé should also list where you went to school and what degrees you hold. If you graduated from high school, you should indicate this, and if you have not yet graduated, indicate your expected graduation date. If you got your general

RESUME

10 High Street
Jobsville

01234 567890

...mployment as a software deve...

...rs IT development experienc...
...dly, flexible, and pro-active r...
...essful at customer facing wo...
...r for creativity and design
...ensive Internet and Intranet

...ent History

...veloper, Computer Comp:

...ember in the software tear...
...ch technology. I have dev...
..., covering all stages of the
... for project management :

...omplishments

...Produced state of the art
...Developed several web t
...techniques
...Successfully project ma
...to installation
...Delivered bespoke sol
...Ported software ont v
...Developed of compa
...Full development of

...ware Engineer, Softv

...orked as both a perma
...oducts on various plat'
...veloping the compan'
...ght deadlines.

...Engineer, !

Mr John Doe
The Company
Anothertown
Anothercity
12345

Dear Mr Doe

I am a junior majoring in Computer Science at University. I re...
Jones, a Control Designer in your organisation. He recommend...
resume to your attention. I would appreciate if you accepted th...
aforementioned resume as an application for an intern position

Over the past few semesters, I have taken several classes that...
background in digital design. These courses familiarized me with...
to abstract and organize complex computational devices and bel...
their models. In addition, I gained experience in low-level circuit...
techniques.

My last internship at Computer Corporation provided me with an...
a significant contribution to a large, dynamic project. While on th...
team, I learned to coordinate my individual efforts with the other...
people around me. I developed strong organizational and team o...
confident that these abilities would serve me well on your design

As stated earlier, I am very interested in integrated circuits and fe...
contribute to the efforts of your design team. I would appreciate t...
discuss my qualifications and your summer employment opportun...
I can be contacted at 555-246-1234. I look forward to hearing fro...

Thank you.

Sincerely,

Ann Another

A good cover letter should follow a very specific form. Use this opportunity to demonstrate your qualifications and enthusiasm for the position, as well as your knowledge of the company or organization to which you are applying.

equivalency degree (or GED), you should also indicate this on your résumé. If you have taken any relevant college courses, you should put these on your résumé as well.

Try to keep the résumé short and concise. Ideally it should not exceed a page in length. If you are having trouble with this, remember that you don't have to include everything you have ever done. Emphasize positions you have held recently or positions that would particularly qualify you for a career in sanitation work. For example, a job as a pizza delivery person would be more relevant to sanitation work than a job making pizza in the kitchen because it demonstrates you are used to driving as part of your job and can learn the ins-and-outs of an area's geography and roadways.

When writing your résumé, seek advice from a trusted teacher, counselor, or family member. The more sets of eyes that review your résumé, the more likely that any mistakes will be caught, guaranteeing that you will put your best foot forward. You might even consider taking your résumé to a trained résumé consultant at a career assistance center.

Whenever you submit your résumé or apply for a job of any kind, you should always include a cover letter. The cover letter can mean the difference between getting an interview and having your résumé be ignored. The cover letter shouldn't just repeat what your résumé says. It should add a personal touch. It is often your first contact with a potential employer. As such, it is your best chance to make a good first impression and get your résumé to stand out among all the other applicants. An effective cover letter should explain the reasons why you are interested in the position and what skills and experiences you have that would make you a good fit for the job. Your cover level should express a high level of interest and knowledge about the position. Like the résumé, it is very important that your cover letter have no typos or grammatical errors. Have an extra set of eyes review it to check for errors.

Whether you apply for a position online or by directly sending your résumé and cover letter to a hiring agent, your hope is the same: that you will get an interview and have a real chance to meet with someone. During the interview, you can convince him or her in person, face-to-face, of what an excellent candidate you are for a position in sanitation work.

CHAPTER FOUR

The Interview Process

After all the legwork, research, applications, test taking, and networking, getting an interview might feel like the last step in the job search process. While getting an interview is a huge step and something you should be proud of, it does not mean that you have the job. It is important to take the interview as seriously as every other step in the process. It can mean the difference between receiving a job offer and going home empty-handed to start the process all over again. This doesn't mean that you should be nervous about an interview. Be confident in your abilities and the fact that they wouldn't have invited you in for an interview if they didn't already think you were qualified.

Before the interview, all those who are in charge of hiring know about you is what you have written about yourself in the documents you provided. They can see the previous jobs you have included on your résumé, your test scores, and (assuming you submitted a cover letter) a little about your interest in the job. The interview is the first chance for them to really get a sense of who you are as a person.

The interview will help those who are making hiring decisions resolve any questions they may have whose answers can't be found in your application materials alone. Are you

An interview is a chance for you to reveal the confident, respectful, industrious, and responsible individual you are. It puts a human face to your résumé, allows you to forge a personal connection with the interviewer, and offers the opportunity to distinguish yourself from the competition.

confident and enthusiastic about the position? Does your personality seem like one that would mesh well with the rest of the team? (This is particularly important in sanitation work because each employee must be a team player for the

DRESSING FOR SUCCESS

You may have heard the saying, "You only get one chance to make a first impression." The interview is your chance to make your first impression a good one. The first thing the interviewer will notice about you is what you're wearing.

You might think because you will be working in the sanitation industry and because the on-the-job dress code will likely be casual that you can show up wearing whatever you like. However, the way you dress demonstrates how seriously you take the interview. If you show up looking like you just rolled out of bed, the interviewer will sense that you don't take the interview seriously. Your clothes should be clean and well-pressed. You should wear a button-down shirt and a pair of slacks. Women can wear dress slacks or a conservative dark skirt. Men should wear a belt and a conservative tie. Wear dress shoes rather than sneakers and, for women, low heels or flats rather than high heels.

Aside from your clothes, your overall appearance should be polished. Your hair should be brushed and your face either clean-shaven or with facial hair that is neatly trimmed. Women should avoid long and heavily decorated nails.

By taking the time to present yourself in a positive way, you send a message to the interviewer that you are confident and sincerely interested in the position.

When you go to an interview, be sure to dress the part. Not only will you indicate to the interviewer that you take the opportunity seriously, but you will feel more confident and prepared.

operation to run smoothly.) Are you intelligent, articulate, and competent? Your answers to the interviewer's direct questions will only be part of the interview. The other part will be based on the impression you make: how you dress, how you carry yourself, and what kind of personality you project. It is important to make a good first impression even before the moment you walk in the door.

Before the Interview

A good first impression doesn't just start when you walk in the door. You should begin creating that positive first impression the night before by getting a good night's sleep. Go to bed early to make sure you will be well-rested and refreshed on the day of the interview. In addition to getting a good night's sleep, make sure to eat a nutritious breakfast or lunch (depending on your interview time) on the day of the interview. You don't want anything—such

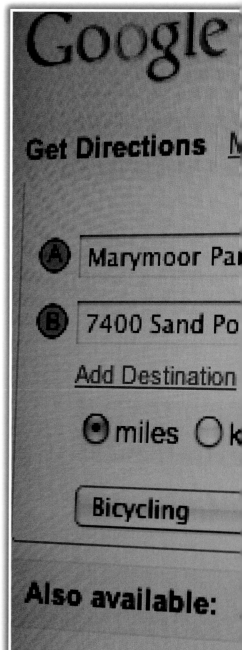

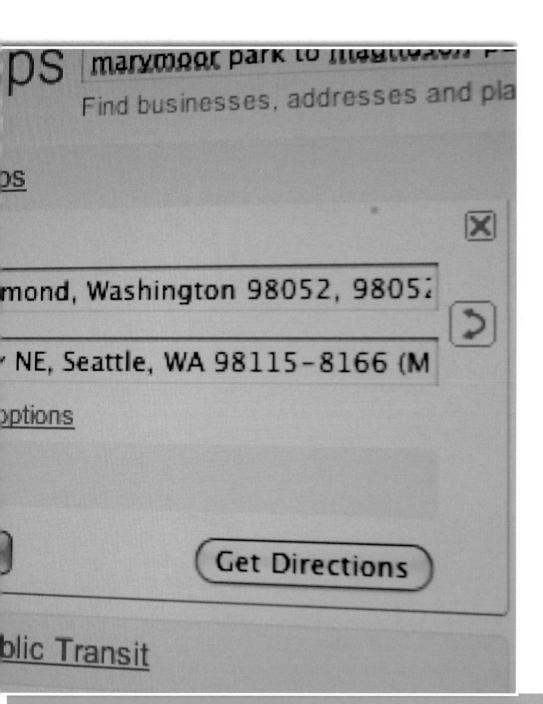

Looking up directions to your interview site the day before will help ensure that you don't get lost or stressed out trying to find it minutes before the interview is scheduled to begin.

as fatigue or hunger—to distract you from doing your best at the interview.

If your interview is in the morning, it is a good idea to write down directions for how to get there the night before. Make sure to allow plenty of time to arrive at the interview site because you never know if public transportation or traffic might delay you. If the interview is being held in a part of town you have never been to or you aren't sure about the exact location, you might want to do a trial run and head over the day before. That way you won't be stressed out about finding the location right before the interview. The more stress you can remove from the interview process, the better. Also, showing up on time, or ideally ten minutes early, shows you are interested in the job, take the interview seriously, and respect the interviewer's valuable time.

When you go to the interview, you should make sure to bring a few copies of your résumé with you. You don't necessarily know how many people you will be meeting with, and some or all of them might not already have a printed copy of your résumé. Being able to hand them a clean, crisp copy proves you are prepared and will give them something to reference when asking you questions.

Practice interviewing at home before the interview. Look up some common interview questions and figure out what your answers to them would be. Sample questions might be: "Why do you want to work here?" or "What do you consider your greatest strengths as an applicant?" You might want to ask a friend or family member to run through a mock interview with you. This will give you practice answering questions on the spot. If during your networking and research phase you had any luck finding someone who works in the

The more you can research and rehearse before your interview, the better prepared you will be for it. Try to anticipate what questions the interviewer might ask and how you would respond.

sanitation industry, he or she will be able to give you a good idea of what questions an interviewer might ask.

During the Interview

You will want to arrive ten minutes early to the interview. It is always good policy to add some extra cushion just in case you are running late. Showing up late to an interview shows bad time-management skills and suggests that you are not taking the interview seriously.

During the job interview, try to relax and stay as calm as possible. After a question is asked, take a moment to gather your thoughts. Maintain eye contact with the interviewer. Listen to the entire question before you answer—you never want to interrupt the interviewer. Also, make sure to pay very close attention to the question being asked and answer accordingly. The best thing you can do is to be yourself and avoid nervousness. Be professional and polite, but ultimately let your personality demonstrate that you are a responsible and hard worker who would get along well with fellow team members.

So what are some mistakes you can make that might count against you in the interview? Aside from arriving late and poorly dressed, these are some things you should absolutely never do in an interview:

- Never answer your phone, check it for messages, or text in the presence of the interviewer. Silence your phone before entering the building, and keep it out of sight throughout the interview.
- Never zone out during the interview. Make sure to make eye contact, ask questions, and practice active listening.

Getting distracted and asking your interviewer to repeat a question makes you look scattered and inattentive.

• Never badmouth anyone, especially a boss, from your current job or at any place you've worked in the past.

• Never talk for too long in answering a question that requires a concise and specific answer. Avoid getting off topic. Answer questions fully, but don't waste the interviewer's time with too much rambling. On the other hand, avoid "yes" and "no" answers. Follow up each "yes" or "no" with a brief explanation of the reasons behind your response.

After the Interview

After you've left the building and the interview is officially over, there is still one important step left to complete. It is very important to follow up with the interviewer and make sure he or she knows that you are grateful for the opportunity to meet and that you are very interested in the position. Taking the time to follow up with a thank-you note after an interview will reinforce that you are a strong candidate for the position. The best way to contact people after the interview is through e-mail. This way they will get your note quickly. Send the note as soon as you get a chance after the interview. You should send an individual e-mail to each person you met with during the interview. After meeting each person, ask if he or she has a business card. Business cards contain contact information like phone numbers, street addresses, and e-mail addresses that you can use to direct your follow-up correspondence to the correct location.

So what should you include in this follow-up note? Keep the note short and to the point. You can use this opportunity

After your interview, make sure to send a follow-up e-mail to thank the interviewers for their time and reiterate your interest in the position.

to repeat your interest in the job and the industry. You can also mention anything you wished you had said during the interview but didn't. Most important, you should thank the interviewer for his or her time in meeting with you and for his or her consideration of your application. As with all professional letters, make sure to proofread your note carefully before hitting "send."

After following up, your next step, which can sometimes be the hardest, is to sit and wait for an e-mail or call offering you the job. While it can be hard to sit and wait by the phone, try not to check in and follow up with the interviewer too often. There is a fine line between interest in the job and pestering. If you do get a job offer, however: congratulations! Now the real work can begin. The next chapter will look at what the first few weeks of your job as a new sanitation worker might be like.

CHAPTER FIVE

Learning the Ropes

W hen you finally receive a job offer and get ready to start your first day on the job, it can be very exciting. It can also be nerve-racking, as you know you will be meeting many new people and learning important tasks, rules, and policies. But there's no reason to be nervous. You've gotten this far because you meet all of the qualifications for the job and you have impressed those who are doing the hiring. All you have to do is pay attention, learn the on-the-job skills that are required, and follow instructions. Show up well-rested and ready to work. If you were told to follow a particular dress code, make sure you are dressed exactly according to the rules. Make sure to give yourself plenty of time to get to your new job—you don't want to be late on your first day.

Orientation and Training

The first thing you will probably do when you start your new job is to undergo an orientation During the orientation, you may meet with your boss or someone from human resources who will outline important policies that you will need to be aware of and rules you will need to follow. He or she may also tell you about health care and retirement benefits that you will receive as a full-time sanitation worker. Don't be afraid to take notes and ask questions during the orientation. It is

Your training includes learning about the equipment you will use on the job. Some of the equipment and vehicles are complicated and dangerous, so it's very important to pay very careful attention during the training sessions.

important that you know and understand all the rules, guide-lines, policies, and benefits of your department.

Many cities will have an orientation or training period that lasts for around two weeks. You will be paid during this

Sanitation workers don't just clear away trash. They perform equally important tasks like de-icing and snow removal to make roads safe for winter driving.

training period because learning about the job is just as important a part of your work as actually doing it. The training you will undergo during this time is usually a combination of classroom training, equipment training, and driving instruction.

Classroom training involves reviewing the rules and regulations of the department as well as your benefits. Equipment training consists of hands-on experience with all of the tools, machines, and vehicles you will be operating while on the job. These may include garbage collection trucks and street sweepers. During this part of your training, you will be taught special driving techniques that are specific to the kinds of vehicles you will be driving and operating.

Pay and Benefits

Many sanitation workers, especially those who are in a union, have excellent benefits. If you are working directly for the government, you have union-set wages. These wages are usually paid by the hour, rather

ON THE JOB WITH A SANITATION WORKER

When the alarm rings at 4 AM, sanitation worker Mark jumps to his feet. He will already be hard at work before the sun is up and before many people are even awake. He puts on his uniform: a bright neon orange vest over his jeans and shirt. This will make sure he is highly visible on the streets to passing cars, even while it is still dark out. He drives to where he will meet his team and pick up his truck.

Mark and his team have been doing this route together for long enough that they know exactly where they are going. Mark is not driving today, but instead is riding on the back of the truck. He jumps down to collect trash bags people have left out on the curb. Mark always wears gloves—after all, he never knows when a bag might contain something sharp or toxic that could hurt his hands. Many bags are light and well-sealed, and he tosses them into the truck with a practiced hand. Others are more of a challenge because garbage was crammed into the bags without much concern for the people who would later be carting it off. The worst is wet cat litter. After a rainstorm, it becomes as heavy as cement.

But Mark can't complain too much. It's a sunny day, and he's outside to enjoy it. His shift ends in the afternoon when his route is completed. He waves good-bye to his team and heads home to shower and enjoy the rest of his day.

The day-to-day job of sanitation workers can vary depending on where and for whom they work. Many sanitation workers have an assigned route they routinely follow to pick up all the trash put out for them to collect.

than a lump-sum annual salary. You're likely to work a five-day week. You might also have the potential for overtime because public works staff often gets pressed into duty to help out during blizzards. Garbage truck drivers can also double as

Sanitation workers often work extra hours and make overtime pay during busy collection times, such as after severe storms, autumn leaf cleanup, or holidays.

snowplow or sanding/salting truck drivers. If you work overtime hours, it means you will get paid more for each hour you work on top of your normal hourly wage.

Other benefits include paid vacation time and sick days,

health insurance, and a retirement plan. Although the health insurance and retirement plan won't likely begin on your first day of employment, it is still important for you to learn as much as you can about them. If you are given a brochure, read it extremely carefully. And, if you have a chance to meet with a health insurance or retirement plan representative, make sure to draw up a list of any questions you have so that he or she can answer them. If you're not working for a government but for a private firm, your salary and benefits may work somewhat differently. Private companies often pay a bit better but have fewer benefits. Either way, the same advice applies: Pay attention, take notes, and ask questions if you don't understand what you're being told.

Being a Team Player

After you complete your orientation and training, you will likely be assigned a collection route. You will usually be given a chance to alternate between driving and the actual collecting of garbage to make sure you develop the necessary skills for all the tasks that are a part of your job. You will likely be placed on a team with sanitation workers who have been doing the job for a while. That way your team members can continue your training once you're on the job by answering any questions you might have. And by showing you how it's done, you get to know the drill.

Any job you ever have will likely involve working with other people. Whether you are working in an office or a restaurant, you have to learn to operate as a team in order to complete your work effectively and efficiently. As a sanitation worker, getting along with coworkers is especially important. The job is dangerous and fast-paced, so if someone makes a mistake, it puts the whole team in peril.

If you have seen sanitation workers on the job collecting

Sanitation worker can be a rewarding career choice. You can support yourself and your family doing something active and engaging, all while providing an essential service to people everywhere.

garbage in your neighborhood, you might notice that they seem to operate like a well-oiled machine. Usually one person will drive and one or two others will ride on the back of the truck and jump off to empty people's trash cans into the truck. The people on the back of the truck have to trust that the driver will do his or her job and not drive recklessly. The people emptying trashcans must work as a team to transfer trash from the cans to the truck in the fastest, safest, most thorough, and most efficient way possible. As you can see, teamwork and trust are very important for sanitation workers.

For this reason, it is very important that you make a good first impression on your new coworkers. Be polite and confident. Don't tell any jokes that might offend anyone. You should be friendly and make an effort to get to know the people you will be working with, but don't forget that your priority is to learn the ropes and do the best job possible. Your coworkers are more likely to like and respect you if they know you have their back and won't let them down out on the streets. Working on a team means realizing that your own work and job safety practices don't affect only you, but also the people you work with. Be safe, responsible, and a hard worker, and you will quickly become a well-liked and highly valued member of the team.

Being a sanitation worker isn't for everyone. It's a difficult job that requires a lot of physical energy. However, like firefighters or police officers, sanitation workers are an essential part of any city or town's health, safety, and smooth functioning. After all, they make it possible for people to live close to each other in great numbers without spreading disease. It is a job that makes a difference in people's lives even if they don't always recognize, appreciate, or properly value it. By becoming a sanitation worker, you aren't just choosing a job, but pursuing a career. With regular raises and generous benefits, it is a career that can offer you a promising and stable future. Not everyone has what it takes to be a sanitation worker, but hopefully now you have enough information to decide if it is the right choice for you.

career assistance center A public help organization that may offer services like career counseling and résumé review.

CDL A commercial driver's license; required for being able to legally drive certain vehicles.

cholera An infectious and often fatal disease caused by bacteria. Cholera is common in areas with poor sanitation.

civil service The administrative service of a government, one in which appointments are determined by competitive examination.

civil service exam A test taken by people who want to be government workers.

commercial Of or relating to a business or markets and the buying and selling of goods and services.

cover letter A letter that is sent with a résumé or other document that serves to introduce that document. When job applicants send résumés to a prospective employer, they should send a cover letter with each one.

dysentery A disease that results from bacteria or parasites. Dysentery is common in areas with poor sanitation.

fluency The ability to speak or write in a language nearly as well as a native speaker.

GED General equivalency diploma; a qualification equal to graduating from high school.

hazardous Risky; dangerous; toxic.

health insurance A benefit offered by a place of employment to its workers that can help them pay medical expenses.

interview The process of meeting with and being evaluated by the person in charge of hiring for a job.

labor strike A refusal to work for owners or management until worker demands are met or a compromise is reached through a bargaining process.

networking The process of using personal and professional connections to help you find a job, give you information about an industry, or further your career advancement.

orientation A period during which you are introduced to your new job, its procedures, its policies, and the workplace.

pension A retirement fund to which both the employee and employer contribute.

résumé A document that summarizes your background, education, skills, and job experience.

sanitation Conditions related to public health, especially methods for adequate waste and sewage disposal.

union A group of workers who band together to seek the same goals for salary, benefits, job security, working conditions, and career advancement.

American Society of Civil Engineers (ASCE)
1801 Alexander Bell Drive
Reston, VA 20191
(800) 548-2723
Web site: http://www.asce.org
Founded in 1852, the American Society of Civil Engineers represents more than 140,000 members of the civil engineering profession worldwide, including sanitation workers. It is America's oldest national engineering society.

Canadian Labour Congress
2841 Riverside Drive
Ottawa, ON K1V 8X7
Canada
(613) 521-3400
Web site: http://canadianlabour.ca
With over 3.3 million members, the Canadian Labour Congress is the largest democratic and popular organization. It brings together Canada's national and international unions, including those that represent the interests of Canadian sanitation workers throughout the provincial and territorial federations of labor and 130 district labor councils.

City of New York Department of Sanitation
Central Correspondence Unit
346 Broadway, 10th Floor
New York, NY 10013
(212) 788-8010
Web site: http://www.nyc.gov/html/dsny

The New York Department of Sanitation has been around since 1881, when it was founded as the Department of Street Cleaning. Today, the department is the world's largest, collecting over 10,500 tons of residential and institutional refuse and 1,760 tons of recyclables a day.

Human Resources and Skills Development Canada
Canada Enquiry Centre
Ottawa, ON K1A 0J9
Canada
(800) 563-5677
Web site: http://www.hrsdc.gc.ca
A division of the Canadian government, Human Resources and Skills Development Canada is committed to career help for Canadian citizens. It provides job assistance, career advice, and a number of other services.

International Brotherhood of Teamsters
25 Louisiana Avenue NW
Washington, DC 20001
(202) 624-6800
Web site: http://www.teamster.org
The Teamsters are America's largest and most diverse labor union. They have been around since 1803 and have organized workers in virtually every occupation imaginable, both professional and nonprofessional, private sector and public sector, including sanitation workers.

Occupational Safety and Health Administration (OSHA)
200 Constitution Avenue NW
Washington, DC 20210

(800) 321-OSHA (6742)
Web site: http://www.osha.gov
OSHA assures safe and healthful working conditions for
    working men and women by setting and enforcing stan-
    dards and by providing training, outreach, education, and
    assistance.

Outdoor Industry Association (OIA)
4909 Pearl East Circle, Suite 300
Boulder, CO 80301
(303) 444-3353
Web site: http://www.outdoorindustry.org/careercenter.html
Founded in 1989, the OIA is the premier trade association
    for companies in the active outdoor recreation business.
    The Outdoor Industry Career Center is the premier
    resource for outdoor jobs and career connections in the
    outdoor industry. It offers one of the most comprehen-
    sive career and recruiting sites, matching qualified
    candidates with a passion for the outdoors to the top
    employers in the industry.

U.S. Department of Labor Employment and Training
    Administration (ETA)
Frances Perkins Building
200 Constitution Avenue NW
Washington, DC 20210
(877) 872-5627
Web site: http://www.doleta.gov
The ETA administers federal government job training and
    helps workers find jobs. It does this largely through the
    local and state organizations under its watch.

U.S. Equal Employment Opportunity Commission (EEOC)
131 M Street NE
Washington, DC 20507
(202) 663-4900
Web site: http://www.eeoc.gov
The EEOC is responsible for enforcing federal laws that make it illegal to discriminate against a job applicant or an employee because of the person's race, color, religion, sex (including pregnancy), national origin, age (forty or older), disability, or genetic information. It is also illegal to discriminate against a person because the person complained about discrimination, filed a charge of discrimination, or participated in an employment discrimination investigation or lawsuit. The laws apply to all types of work situations, including hiring, firing, promotions, harassment, training, wages, and benefits.

Web Sites

Due to the changing nature of Internet links, Rosen Publishing has developed an online list of Web sites related to the subject of this book. This site is updated regularly. Please use this link to access the list:

http://www.rosenlinks.com/JOBS/Sani

FOR FURTHER READING

Axman, Melanie. *A Short Guide to Editing Your Résumé*. Seattle, WA: Amazon Digital Services, 2012.

Bennington, Emily, and Skip Lineberg. *Effective Immediately: How to Fit In, Stand Out, and Move Up at Your First Real Job*. New York, NY: Ten Speed Press, 2010.

Beshara, Tony. *Unbeatable Résumés: America's Top Recruiters Reveal What Really Gets You Hired*. New York, NY: AMACOM, 2011.

Bolles, Mark Emery, and Richard Bolles. *Job Hunting Online*. New York, NY: Ten Speed Press, 2008.

Burns, Daniel. *The First 60 Seconds: Win the Job Interview Before It Begins*. Naperville, IL: Sourcebooks, 2009.

Christensen, Thomas. *Solid Waste Technology and Management*. Hoboken, NJ: Wiley, 2010.

Doyle, Allison. *Internet Your Way to a New Job*. Cupertino, CA: Happy About, 2011.

Hill, Paul. *The Panic Free Job Search: Unleash the Power of the Web and Social Networking to Get Hired*. Pompton Plains, NJ: Career Press, 2012.

Lyden, Mark. *College Students: Do This! Get Hired!: From Freshman to Ph.D.: The Secrets, Tips, Techniques, and Tricks You Need to Get the Full-Time Job, Co-op, or Summer Internship Position You Want*. Charleston, SC: BookSurge Publishing, 2009.

Macken, JoAnn Early. *Sanitation Workers* (People in My Community). New York, NY: Gareth Stevens Publishing, 2010.

Mayer, Dale. *Career Essentials: The Résumé*. Spring City, PA: Valley Publishing, 2011.

Misner, Ivan, et al. *Networking Like a Pro: Turning Contacts into Connections*. Irvine, CA: Entrepreneur Press, 2010.

Nagle, Robin. *Picking Up: On the Streets and Behind the Trucks with the Sanitation Workers of New York City.* New York, NY: Farrar, Straus and Giroux, 2013.

Oxlade, Chris. *Garbage and Recycling.* Mankato, MN: Heinemann-Raintree. 2012.

Reeves, Ellen Gordon. *Can I Wear My Nose Ring to the Interview?: A Crash Course in Finding, Landing, and Keeping Your First Real Job.* New York, NY: Workman Publishing Company, 2009.

Zack, Devora. *Networking for People Who Hate Networking: A Field Guide for Introverts, the Overwhelmed, and the Underconnected.* San Francisco, CA: Berrett-Koehler, 2010.

Adler, Oscar. *Sell Yourself in Any Interview: Use Proven Sales Techniques to Land Your Dream Job.* New York, NY: McGraw-Hill, 2009.

Believer magazine. "Interview with Robin Nagle." September 2010. Retrieved August 2012 (http://believermag.com/issues/201009/?read=interview_nagle).

Bolles, Mark Emery, and Richard Bolles. *Job Hunting Online.* New York, NY: Ten Speed Press, 2008.

Burns, Daniel. *The First 60 Seconds: Win the Job Interview Before It Begins.* Naperville, IL: Sourcebooks, 2009.

City of Chicago. "Streets and Sanitation." Retrieved August 2012 (http://www.cityofchicago.org/city/en/depts/streets.html).

City of Los Angeles. "Sanitation: Department of Public Works." Retrieved August 2012 (http://www.lacitysan.org).

City of New York. "Department of Sanitation: New York City." Retrieved August 2012 (http://www.nyc.gov/html/dsny/html/jobs/jobs.shtml).

Learning Express editors. *The Complete Preparation Guide for the Sanitation Worker Exam, New York City.* New York, NY: Learning Express, 2009.

Logan, Joseph. *Seven Simple Steps to Landing Your First Job.* Boulder, CO: Maytown Press, 2010.

Lubin, Gus, and Kevin Lincoln. "The 15 Most Dangerous Jobs in America." *Business Insider*, September 21, 2011. Retrieved August 2012 (http://articles.businessinsider.com/2011-09-21/news/30183469_1_fisherman-dangerous-jobs-fatality-rate).

Mihelcic, James R., and Lauren Fry. *Field Guide to Environmental Engineering for Development Workers: Water, Sanitation, and*

Indoor Air. Reston, VA: American Society of Civil Engineers, 2009.

Nagle, Robin. "Entry 1." Slate.com, October 4, 2004. Retrieved August 2012 (http://www.slate.com/articles/ arts_and_life/diary/features/2004/_3/entry_1.html).

Provenzano, Steve. *Blue Collar Resumes*. Independence, KY: Course Technology PTR/Cengage Learning, 2012.

Roza, Greg. *Great Networking Skills*. New York, NY: Rosen Publishing, 2008.

Vaughn, Jacqueline. *Waste Management: A Reference Handbook*. Santa Barbara, CA: ABC-CLIO, 2008.

About the Author

Susan Meyer is a writer living and working in New York City, home to one of the largest systems of organized sanitation in the world. She has written a number of previous titles for Rosen Publishing.

Photo Credits